YOU CHO

T0011058

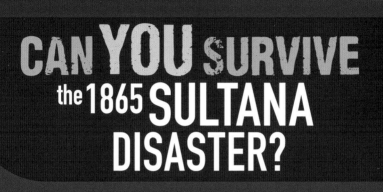

CAN YOU SURVIVE
the 1865 SULTANA
DISASTER?

AN INTERACTIVE HISTORY ADVENTURE

by Eric Braun

CAPSTONE PRESS
a capstone imprint

Published by Capstone Press, an imprint of Capstone.
1710 Roe Crest Drive
North Mankato, Minnesota 56003
capstonepub.com

Library of Congress Cataloging-in-Publication Data.
Names: Braun, Eric, 1971- author.
Title: Can you survive the Sultana disaster? : an interactive history adventure /
  by Eric Braun.
Other titles: You choose books. Disasters in history.
Description: North Mankato, Minnesota : Capstone Press, a Capstone imprint,
  [2023] | Series: You choose. Disasters in history | "Choices: 41; endings: 22." |
  Includes bibliographical references. | Audience: Ages 8-12 | Audience: Grades 4-6
Summary: "The date is April 27, 1865. You are crammed onboard the steamboat
  Sultana with more than 2,000 passengers. Many of them are soldiers heading
  home after the Civil War. You're cruising on the Mississippi River when a massive
  explosion rips through the ship. Do you dive into the water to save yourself or stay
  onboard to help the survivors? Will you try to swim for shore or wait for help to
  arrive? Will you stay with your sick friend or try to find someone to help him?
  With dozens of possible choices, it's up to you to decide how you'll survive one of
  the worst river disasters ever seen"—Provided by publisher.
Identifiers: LCCN 2022028939 (print) | LCCN 2022028940 (ebook) |
  ISBN 9781666390858 (library binding) | ISBN 9781666390841 (paperback) |
  ISBN 9781666391008 (ebook pdf)
Subjects: LCSH: Sultana (Steamboat)—Juvenile literature. | Steamboat
  disasters—Mississippi River—Juvenile literature. | Boating accidents—
  Mississippi River—Juvenile literature. | Plot-your-own stories. | United States—
  History—Civil War, 1861-1865—Peace—Juvenile literature. | LCGFT:
  Choose-your-own stories.
Classification: LCC E595.S84 B73 2023 (print) | LCC E595.S84 (ebook) |
  DDC 973.7/71—dc23/eng/20220708
LC record available at https://lccn.loc.gov/2022028939
LC ebook record available at https://lccn.loc.gov/2022028940

Editorial Credits
Editor: Aaron Sautter; Designer: Bobbie Nuytten; Media Researcher: Donna
Metcalf; Production Specialist: Whitney Schaefer

All internet sites appearing in back matter were available and accurate when this
book was sent to press.

Printed and bound in the USA. PO#5195

TABLE OF CONTENTS

ABOUT YOUR ADVENTURE

It is the end of the U.S. Civil War (1861–1865). YOU are a Union soldier who was captured by the South and sent to a prison camp. You've been dreaming of going home for a long time.

As you get on board the steamboat *Sultana*, you can almost feel your own pillow against your cheek. But a disaster is about to occur during your journey. Will you make it home to your family safely?

Chapter One sets the scene. Then you choose which path to read. Follow the directions at the bottom of the page as you read the stories. The decisions you make determine what happens next. After you finish one path, go back and read the others for new perspectives and more adventures.

Turn the page to begin your adventure.

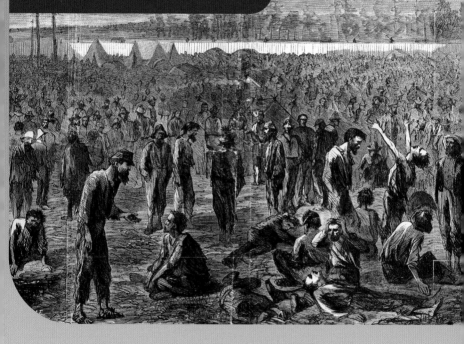
Conditions in Confederate prisoner of war camps were often crowded and dirty. Many prisoners died from starvation and disease.

CHAPTER 1
THE LONG VOYAGE HOME

After four bloody, brutal years, the North has won the war. Soldiers all over the country are on the move and heading home.

For you, the journey began in a prison camp. You were captured and imprisoned by a Confederate army unit. There you waited out the end of the fighting in terrible conditions. Many of the prisoners suffered from diseases. Food and medicine were almost impossible to get.

Now you are free, but the road home hasn't been easy. You've traveled hundreds of miles and made your way to the port town of Vicksburg, Mississippi.

Turn the page.

There, a steamboat will take you north up the Mississippi River to Union headquarters in Ohio. Then you'll be processed and sent home. You've been traveling for weeks, but you still have a long journey ahead of you.

When you arrive in Vicksburg, you go to Camp Fisk at the edge of town. The camp is crowded with hundreds of soldiers. Some are as young as 14. Others are seasoned officers. There are even some Confederate soldiers. You check in with authorities at the camp, and they give you clean clothes and a hot meal. You are deeply grateful for both.

That night, you chat with other soldiers. Everyone is exhausted from the war. Many are wounded or sick. But they're all excited to be going home.

While talking to a group of men by a fire pit, you learn that President Abraham Lincoln has been assassinated. The news is devastating. The president led the country through its worst crisis, only to be killed when it was over. It fills you with sadness.

Turn the page.

After President Lincoln's death, funeral processions were held in several cities before his body was buried in Springfield, Illinois.

You also learn more about the riverboat you'll be sailing on. "The *Sultana*," says an older soldier with a crutch and a bloody leg. "I'm on that one, too, I'm afraid."

"Why are you afraid?" you ask. The fire crackles between you.

"Word going round is that one of the boilers has a leak," the man says, scratching his filthy beard.

"Good luck," says another man. "I hear they're just patching it instead of a full repair."

"They wouldn't let us on if it wasn't safe, would they?" you ask.

"I don't know," the man with the crutch says. He chuckles softly. "But if that boat doesn't leave by tomorrow, the captain stands to lose a lot of money."

You don't sleep well that night. Partly because you don't have a tent or blanket, and it's a cold April night. But your mind is swimming with thoughts of the president's death and worries about the boat's patched boiler.

However, in the morning you're called to board the *Sultana,* and your worries melt away. The thought of finally sleeping in your own bed back home helps calm your nerves.

To be a teenager from Kentucky, turn to page 13.

To be an officer returning to Michigan, turn to page 41.

To be a Union soldier from Tennessee, turn to page 11.

Andersonville Prison in Georgia kept as many as 45,000 Union soldiers as prisoners.

CHAPTER 2
THE KENTUCKY KID

You were only 14 years old when you joined the Army. Kids your age weren't allowed to fight. But you felt strongly that the cause of the North was important. So you lied about your age and signed up.

You saw many battles and many horrors on the battlefield. But perhaps nothing you saw was as awful as what you witnessed in the terrible Andersonville prison camp. After being captured in battle, you spent the last months of the war here, including your sixteenth birthday.

The prison camp was just a walled-in rectangle of land. Thousands of men were crammed inside, most of them as thin as skeletons. There was rarely any food to eat.

Turn the page.

In the center of the camp was a foul, swampy area where people went to the bathroom. The prisoners had lice and maggots living on them. And flies buzzed constantly. You could hear the moans of men in pain. Many wished they were dead. Along the walls, Confederate soldiers stood ready to shoot anyone who approached them.

After being freed, you traveled a long way to reach Vicksburg. You stuck with your friend Jennings, who was in prison with you. Though he got out of the camp with you, he barely survived. Now he's shivering with fever and can barely walk.

Thankfully, your journey starts on a train. You ride for several hours, but in the middle of Mississippi, it has to stop. The tracks have been blown apart. You are forced to walk the rest of the way. You take it slow and give Jennings several breaks. After all you've been through, he is your best friend. You'd never leave him.

When you finally arrive in Vicksburg, you are given a hot meal. It helps revive Jennings's strength—and yours. In the morning, the two of you get on board the boat.

However, the boat is extremely crowded. You see a clear space near a wall where Jennings can lean back and rest. It looks warmer and less windy there, too. But it is near the back of the boat—a long walk through a thick crowd. Jennings looks to where you're pointing and shakes his head. He staggers and sits right there by the railing. The crowd flows past you.

"Hey, get out of the way!" someone growls.

To carry your friend to the back of the boat, turn to page 16.

To sit with Jennings here, turn to page 18.

You can't just sit here where everyone is walking. Besides, Jennings needs some shelter. So you help him to his feet, bend your knees, and hoist him over your shoulder.

People push back against you as you bump into them. Finally, you reach a clear space against the wall and set Jennings down. He leans back and seems to fall asleep instantly.

When you look over, you notice the men sitting next to you are wearing Confederate uniforms. Your hands turn to fists as you think about your horrible experiences in battle and at the prison camp.

The men stare at you with cold eyes. One of them mutters something about Lincoln, and you think they're probably celebrating that he's been killed.

Are you safe here with these men? The war is over. Even so, they don't seem to like you very much. Maybe you should move. But moving Jennings again doesn't seem like a good idea.

To talk with the Confederate soldiers, turn to page 20.

To move your friend again, turn to page 23.

Confederate soldiers in 1862

Jennings needs rest more than anything. It's not worth fighting the crowds just for a bit of warmth. So you pull him out of the way and huddle together near the railing.

Jennings falls asleep soundly for a while. When he wakes, you talk about your homes. You tell him about your sisters and your mom. You can't wait to see them.

"I'm going to ask my sweetheart to marry me," Jennings says. "Her name is Sara."

His smile is interrupted by a violent bout of shivering. He really needs medical care. He falls asleep again, but his breathing is shallow. He's still trembling.

Late that night, Jennings' condition grows worse. You're worried he might die.

You remember seeing a doctor on board earlier. He was with some officers, heading toward the upper deck. He may be able to help your friend. You know you must try, or Jennings could die. The only question is whether you leave Jennings here or take him with you.

To search for the medical officer by yourself, turn to page 24.

To take Jennings with you, turn to page 27.

"Good morning!" you say to the Southern soldiers. You smile, but it feels funny. Just a couple of weeks ago, you all would have been trying to shoot each other.

At first, the men just ignore you. As soldiers continue boarding the boat, the space gets more and more crowded. Soon there is no place left to stand.

When it left port at Vicksburg, Mississippi, the *Sultana* was overloaded with more than 2,000 passengers and crew.

Jennings moans in his sleep, then wakes up coughing. One of the Confederates looks over and holds out his canteen.

"Fresh water," he says.

"Thank you," you say with a nod.

You give the canteen to Jennings to take a drink. Then you hand it back to the soldier.

Finally, the boat leaves the port. You can hear the engine working hard behind the wall you're leaning against. You talk a bit more with the Confederate soldiers. Like you, they're exhausted from the war and look forward to seeing their families.

That evening, the *Sultana* stops in Memphis, Tennessee, and some of the soldiers get off to look around. Later that night, the boat shoves off again. You and Jennings doze against the engine room wall.

Turn the page.

Suddenly, you are awakened by a groaning sound. At first you think it's Jennings, but it's not coming from him. This sound is mechanical. It's coming from the engine room.

Something is wrong. You remember what you heard about the patched boiler. A bolt of fear goes through you, and you stand up quickly. If the boat stops right away, it might help save the engine. You could alert the captain, but you'll have to act quickly. And you'd have to leave Jennings behind.

To run to the pilothouse and alert the captain, turn to page 29.

To ignore the noises, turn to page 31.

You're not comfortable staying next to these Confederates. You pull Jennings to his feet and wrap his arm around your shoulders. You push through the crowd again, not sure where you're going. The boat is so full now that it is standing room only. Maybe you should have stayed where you were. At least you had a place to sit.

Near the stairs to the upper deck, Jennings collapses. You stand next to him to protect him from getting stepped on.

Soon the boat lurches. You realize it's leaving port, and you're glad to finally be moving. But after a few hours, it stops in Memphis, Tennessee. Some of the soldiers are getting off to look around the city. You have a couple hours. You could go look for help for Jennings. But should you leave your friend here by himself?

To go ashore and look for medicine, turn to page 32.
To stay on the boat with Jennings, turn to page 35.

Dragging Jennings upstairs with you wouldn't be good for him, and it would take too long. You tap the shoulder of a nearby soldier in a long coat.

"Pardon me. Will you keep an eye on my friend?" you ask. "I'm going to see if I can get him some help."

The other soldier nods, and you make your way to the top deck, known as the hurricane deck. In the dark, you see a group of officers talking near the pilothouse. The doctor is with them.

"Please help!" you say as you approach them. "My friend on the main deck—I think he's dying."

The doctor looks at you with tired eyes. His face is creased and worn. His uniform is tattered. You know that he has seen even more death and pain than you have.

"You have any money, kid?" he asks.

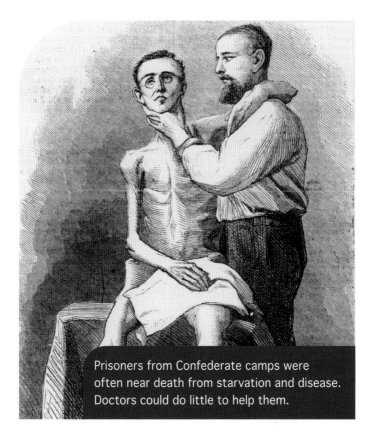

Prisoners from Confederate camps were often near death from starvation and disease. Doctors could do little to help them.

"No," you say. "But he's dying. Please! You have to help."

"Sorry, kid," he says and turns away.

Kid. The word makes you angry. You fought in the same war he did—so what if you're only 16? Maybe if you were older, he would take you seriously.

Turn the page.

But it doesn't matter now. You head back toward Jennings, but before you get there, a huge blast rocks the deck. As the boat lurches, you're thrown against the railing. Your stomach churns as everything turns black.

A few seconds later, you open your eyes. Your head is spinning in a daze.

"Jennings!" you scream. "Where are you?"

Others are screaming, too. You then realize that you're on fire. You scream again for Jennings, but you can't help him even if you found him. You can't even help yourself. You slip off the deck and drop, flaming, into the icy water below.

THE END

To follow another path, turn to page 11.
To learn more about the *Sultana* disaster, turn to page 101.

"Come on, friend," you say, pulling Jennings to his feet.

"I'm too weak. Let me stay here," he says. But you wrap his arm around your shoulder and hoist him to his feet. Together, you shuffle toward the stairs to find the doctor.

You and Jennings are halfway up the steps when you see a flash of fire below you. A split second later comes the sound—KABOOM!

The blast sends you and Jennings flying through the air. You land in the river and come up coughing.

Disoriented, you spot a board from the boat's deck floating near you. You swim to it and hold on. Dozens of feet away, you see Jennings flailing in the water. You know he has little strength left. He's about to drown.

Turn the page.

Fire quickly spread on the Sultana after its boilers exploded.

The river current is pushing you hard in the opposite direction. Still, you might be able to reach Jennings with the board. Then he could rest and possibly survive.

To swim to Jennings with the board, turn to page 37.

To wait and see if he floats to you, turn to page 39.

"I'll be right back," you say to Jennings and then head for the stairs.

When you reach the top deck, there is a giant explosion below you—where you just were. You feel a rush of hot air, and suddenly you are flying up and away from the boat. A streak of orange trails behind you—you're on fire!

You're suddenly encased in a cold darkness. At first you think you're dead. But as bubbles pour from your mouth, you realize that you've been thrown into the river. You surface and look around. Men are screaming and thrashing in the water. Jennings is nowhere to be seen.

You try to stay calm. It's pitch black, except for the fire burning on the boat. You know the river is very wide here. You're at least a couple miles from the shore on either side.

Turn the page.

You swim as hard as you can toward the shore. Luckily, you're an excellent swimmer. You grew up near a small lake where you and your sisters went swimming often. You think of your sisters and how good it will be to see them again. The thought gives you strength as you keep on.

Eventually you reach the shore. You're too tired to climb up the bank, so you lay in the mud and rest. You sadly think of Jennings. You're sure your friend didn't survive. You can hear people yelling and moving through the trees up above you. You close your eyes and wait for them to find you.

THE END

To follow another path, turn to page 11.
To learn more about the *Sultana* disaster, turn to page 101.

You decide there isn't much point in looking for the captain. The engine will either be fine, or it'll break down. There's nothing you can do about it.

You stay next to Jennings and the Confederate soldiers. You swap stories about the war. Of course, they hated the fighting and bloodshed just as much as you did. They might not agree with Lincoln or the Union, but they don't hate you.

"We're all just men," says one of the soldiers.

His shirt is torn away, and he has a weeping wound on his shoulder. He winces when he moves. You reach out to him, and he reaches his good hand out to you. Just as you shake hands, the boat's engine explodes in the room next to you. The soldier's face is the last thing you'll ever see.

THE END

To follow another path, turn to page 11.
To learn more about the *Sultana* disaster,
turn to page 101.

You can't just sit here and do nothing. You decide to go ashore. In the harbor, a woman gives you directions to a doctor, and you're soon standing in the doctor's office. The doctor has a clean, trimmed beard and shiny eyeglasses. You explain Jennings' condition.

"Perhaps quinine?" he says. You know this tonic is sometimes given to people with infections like malaria.

"Yes," you say. "Quinine."

He moves to a small cabinent and takes out a small bottle. "That will be ten cents," he says.

"I don't have any money," you admit.

"Young man," he says, "I know you're trying to help your friend. But I am not in the business of giving away tonics for free."

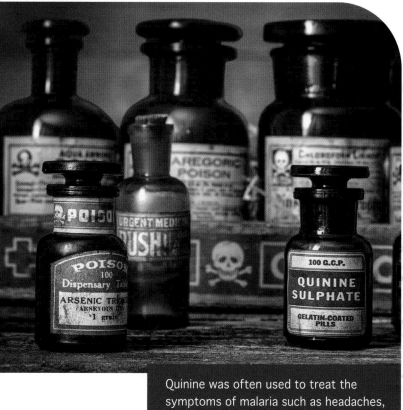

Quinine was often used to treat the symptoms of malaria such as headaches, body aches, fever, chills, and vomiting.

You try to talk the doctor into giving you the medicine, but he refuses. Disappointed, you walk back to the harbor.

Turn the page.

But when you arrive, the ship has left! You took too long. You sit down in the dirt and cry. You feel so alone. You felt like a man fighting the war, but now you're just a little kid. You want to see your mother.

Hours later, you're still sitting in the dirt when you hear someone swimming toward you in the river. "The *Sultana*!" the person says after you help him onto the dock. "It blew up!"

All through the night, you help people get out of the river. After the explosion, they floated in the freezing water downstream back to Memphis. You look for Jennings, hoping to find your friend. But you never see him. You hope he survived somehow, but deep down, you know he's gone.

THE END

To follow another path, turn to page 11.
To learn more about the *Sultana* disaster,
turn to page 101.

You realize that medicine would probably cost money, and you don't have any. You might as well stay with Jennings. Maybe you can keep his spirits up. You ask him questions about his family back home, and he does perk up a bit.

Late that night, you are both dozing when a loud explosion wakes you up. You hold on to the railing as the deck tilts. Your head is bleeding and you feel dizzy. You must have slammed your head against the rail.

Looking down, you see that Jennings has already slid into the water. You drop into the river and swim toward where you last saw him.

At first you can't see him. But then you see one of the Confederate soldiers floating on a piece of the boat's mast. He pulls Jennings up onto it.

Turn the page.

You call out, but neither Jennings nor the Confederate can hear you. You swim toward them, but your head wound is bleeding a lot. The pain is terrible. You get a mouth full of water, and then another.

Within seconds, you feel yourself sinking. You black out, never to open your eyes again.

THE END

To follow another path, turn to page 11.
To learn more about the *Sultana* disaster, turn to page 101.

You're a strong swimmer. You think you can make it. You start kicking your way toward Jennings, pulling the board behind you. But as you draw closer, he dips below the water. He's too weak from his illness and injuries. Before you can reach him, he sinks below the waves.

You dive below the water to look for Jennings. But it's too dark and you can't find him.

Your heart sinks. You know your friend is gone. But you have other things to worry about. How can you stay alive? You can't see the shore—it's miles away in the dark. So, you decide to just hold on to the board, shivering and floating along with the river current. You drift past the remains of the burning boat. People are screaming, and others are thrashing in the water.

Turn the page.

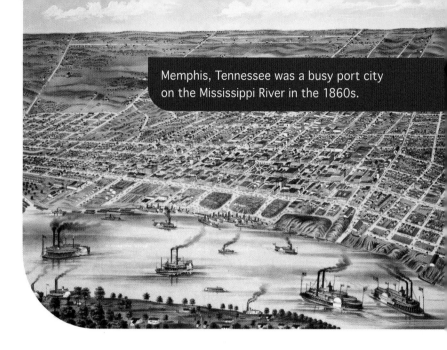

Memphis, Tennessee was a busy port city on the Mississippi River in the 1860s.

Eventually you float all the way back to Memphis. There, you're fished out of the water by some guards. You tell them about the explosion, and they send boats upriver to rescue people. They spend the whole night pulling people out of the water. You couldn't save your friend, but many lives are saved—thanks to you.

THE END

To follow another path, turn to page 11.
To learn more about the *Sultana* disaster, turn to page 101.

"Jennings!" you call out. "Follow my voice! The current will pull you toward me. Fight for your life, Jennings!"

At first it seems like it might work. He splashes toward you. But the current is pulling on you, too. You try to kick your way toward Jennings, but your strength is waning. You see him trying to stay afloat. Before long, you see your friend slip below the surface for good.

Your heart is broken that you couldn't save Jennings. But then you wonder how long you can last yourself. Even this board is no guarantee. It's getting harder to feel your fingers. How much longer can you hold on?

THE END

To follow another path, turn to page 11.
To learn more about the *Sultana* disaster, turn to page 101.

During the Civil War, soldiers rarely got to return home to see their loved ones and families.

CHAPTER 3
AN OFFICER'S JOURNEY

As a lieutenant in the Union Army, you commanded more than 30 men. You served from the earliest moments of the war until the very end. You treated your men well, and they respected you.

A few months ago, you got to visit your wife in Michigan. It was so good to see her, and it reminded you how much you have to live for.

These last few weeks, while in a prison in Texas, were the first time during the whole war that you feared for your life. The diseases spreading in the prison were deadly and relentless. You didn't want to die when the end of the war was so close.

Turn the page.

When you check in at Camp Fisk, an officer gives you a letter. It's from Brigit, your wife. You eagerly open it, and tears spring to your eyes. Brigit is pregnant. You're going to be a father! All the pain and suffering of the war melts away with the good news. You board the *Sultana* in high spirits.

But your mood quickly changes when you see the crowd on the boat. You talk to a soldier from another division, Lieutenant Bronson. His arm is in a dirty, blood-stained sling that hangs beneath his equally stained jacket.

"What's going on here?" you ask him. "This boat can't possibly be safe for this many passengers."

"It's the captain," Bronson says. "He gets paid for every soul he moves up to Ohio. He's bribing the guards in Camp Fisk to keep sending more. I don't like it at all, especially with the news about the boiler leak."

"Yes, I heard about that," you say grimly.

You know that these men all want to go home, just like you. But the situation seems quite dangerous. Perhaps you should talk to the captain. As an officer, you feel you have the authority to do something. On the other hand, nobody else is volunteering to confront the captain. Maybe you shouldn't start a conflict.

To confront the captain about the danger, turn to page 44.

To stick with the other officers, turn to page 47.

None of the other officers are confronting the captain. You know it's not because they think he's doing a good job. They just lack the courage. But you don't.

You leave the others and head upstairs. As you do, you see crew members lifting up the stages. The platforms at the front of the boat allow people and cargo to get on board. You know you'll be leaving soon.

At the wheelhouse, the glassed-in room where the captain steers the boat, a guard stops you at the door.

"I'd like a word with Captain Mason," you tell him. The guard ducks his head inside, speaks a few words to the captain, and invites you inside.

The room is warm and comfortable. Unlike the soldiers and other officers, Captain Mason is clean-shaven and his uniform is clean.

The wheelhouse had windows on all sides so the captain could safely steer the steamboat on the river.

"Sir," you say, saluting the higher-ranked man. "Is the rumor true that there's a boiler leak?"

"The boiler is fine," the captain says.

"But sir," you say. "This boat is well over capacity. The lives of everyone on board are in danger."

Turn the page.

The captain stares at you coldly. Is it anger or mere irritation in his eyes? He says, "You are dismissed, Lieutenant."

"Sir, if I may—"

"I said, dismissed!" he repeats. The guard takes a step toward you. It's clear that the captain doesn't care about the risks. There's too much money to be lost if he holds back.

And then you think of something. There is a lot of money at stake. Why shouldn't you get some of it? He's putting your life in danger, too. What he's doing could get him in trouble—and you both know it.

To threaten to report the captain, turn to page 49.

To follow orders and leave the pilothouse, turn to page 51.

As officers, you're responsible for the men on this ship. You must do everything you can to make sure they make it home safely.

"We must be vigilant," you say to Bronson. "We should stick together. If something goes wrong, we'll have to work together to help all these men."

Bronson looks worried, but he agrees. The two of you stay up on the hurricane deck and watch the river flow by. There was heavy snow this past winter up north, and the river is flooded. The current is strong and fast. You imagine the water must be very cold. The thought of ending up in that water is not comforting.

That night, the boat stops in Memphis, Tennessee, for a couple of hours. You and Bronson watch as some soldiers get off the boat to check out the town. Bronson is nervously twisting his mustache. Finally, he speaks up.

Turn the page.

"Listen," he says. "I've got a bad feeling about this journey. Let's get off the boat."

"What do you mean?" you ask. "Get off—and stay off?"

"Yes," Bronson replies. "We survived a horrible, bloody war. Why should we die now?"

If you get off the boat and don't return, you'll be abandoning your post. The war may be over, but you're still in the Army. You still must follow the rules. You could get into serious trouble for abandoning your post—but only if you're caught.

To go into town, turn to page 53.

To stay on the boat, turn to page 55.

"One last thing," you say nervously. You can't believe you're about to blackmail a superior officer.

Captain Mason sighs in exasperation. "What is it?"

"You need to cut me in on the money, or I'll tell the major what you're doing."

"Oh, really?" the captain says.

"You could go to prison for violating safety protocols and bribing officers. Give me twenty percent of what you're making, and you don't have to worry about it."

"Bribing?" he asks, looking at you suspiciously. He turns to the guard. "Put him in the storage room. And lock it."

"What?" you cry. "You can't do that!"

Turn the page.

But the guard grabs your arm and drags you out of the pilothouse. Another guard joins him, and they lead you down to the hurricane deck. They shove you into a small storage room filled with barrels and crates. Then you hear them lock the door and walk away.

Later that night the engine explodes. You hear people screaming outside, but nobody can hear *your* screams. You're trapped in that room and go down with the boat.

THE END

To follow another path, turn to page 11.
To learn more about the *Sultana* disaster, turn to page 101.

You do as you're told and leave the pilothouse. You wander downstairs to the main deck. By now it's so crowded that everyone is standing shoulder to shoulder. You push your way to the railing near the back of the boat. Behind you is a livestock pen containing horses and cattle.

I bet the captain is being paid for every animal he transports, too, you think. To him, both soldiers and animals are just bodies to help him make money.

Turn the page.

Steamboats often transported horses and other animals on the river.

Sometime after midnight, the boat's boiler explodes. The blast rips a hole through the center of the ship, and flames shoot high into the air.

Many passengers are thrown from the boat. Others are on fire as they run and leap into the water. You are tossed against a wall near the paddle wheel, and pain explodes in your ribs. Then the boat lurches, and you too are thrown into the river.

Your ribs hurt badly—some must be broken. Swimming in the icy water hurts terribly. Peering through the darkness, you make out the shape of a horse swimming nearby. You could try to reach the horse or swim to shore. But in the dark, you're not sure how far the shore is.

To swim for the horse, turn to page 57.
To try to swim for shore, turn to page 59.

Abandoning your post could get you into trouble. But who knows what might happen if you stay on the boat? If the boiler explodes you could be killed. It feels too dangerous to stay on board.

You decide to go into town with Bronson. You both go to a tavern, and although you have no money, the tavern keeper feeds you. Because you're officers, he trusts that you'll repay him when you can. Just as you finish your dinner, you hear the *Sultana* blow its whistle. The boat is leaving. There's no changing your mind now.

That night the tavern keeper lets you stay in a room. You're sound asleep when something wakes you up. Someone is shouting down near the docks. You get up and quickly get dressed to investigate.

At the docks, you see a teenage boy—a Union soldier—talking to some townspeople. He's wet and crying.

Turn the page.

"The *Sultana* exploded!" he says.

You were right to get off the boat! You and Bronson join the boy at the dock. There you see more refugees from the boat floating into the harbor.

"We must help them," Bronson says to you.

You agree that you should help. However, if anyone recognizes you, they'll know that you abandoned the Army.

To help save the *Sultana* refugees, turn to page 61.

To leave and hide, turn to page 63.

"I'm as concerned as you are, Bronson," you say. "But it's our duty to stay at our post."

Bronson doesn't like it, but you convince him to stay on board. "We'll stick together," you say. "It's the best way to stay safe."

You watch from the hurricane deck as soldiers depart the boat and go into Memphis. A couple hours later, they board the boat again, and the *Sultana* leaves the port.

Later, you and Bronson manage to fall asleep on the floor near the stacks. The stacks puff hot engine exhaust out the top. Lying next to them helps you keep warm.

That night you have a beautiful dream. You're playing with your new baby at your home in Michigan. But then you're wakened by a deafening explosion!

Turn the page.

Massive plumes of fire spew from the engine stacks, and you scramble away. A second wave of fire bursts up, and you find yourself clinging to the railing of a burning boat. People everywhere are yelling. Some are running across the deck and jumping into the river below.

You look around for Bronson. You find him clinging to a mast. His feet are hanging over the edge of the deck. Suddenly the boat lurches, and he's tossed off the main deck into the water.

To dive after Bronson,
turn to page 64.

To keep holding on to the railing,
turn to page 67.

You have no idea how far the shore is from here. It might be a mile or two away—too far to swim. It's smarter to swim for the horse. At least it can help you stay afloat for a while.

You reach the horse quickly, and it lets you reach up and lean over its back. The animal is strong, and your weight doesn't seem to affect it. You see Bronson, the officer with the broken arm you talked to earlier.

"Bronson!" you call. "Over here!"

He swims toward you—he's a strong swimmer, even with one arm. Soon he's clinging to the horse's mane with his good hand. The horse makes a nervous-sounding whinny. Its eyes are wild with terror. And no wonder. The burning boat is turning like a merry-go-round on the water. People are screaming and dying all around.

Turn the page.

"Sir!" says a voice. On the other side of the horse is a soldier from your unit.

"Private Carlson," you say. "Are you okay?"

"I'm fine, sir—now that I've found you and this horse. I don't know how to swim well," he says.

But with three of you weighing down the horse, it sinks a bit lower in the water. Its legs are working hard beneath the surface. You're not sure how long the horse can last.

As an officer, you can command Private Carlson to let go. He would almost surely die, but at least you and Bronson would survive. If you all continue to hang on to the horse, you could all drown.

To kick Carlson off the horse, turn to page 68.
To let him stay, turn to page 69.

If you cling to the horse, you'll just stay out here longer. You don't know if anyone will save you. But if you go for the shore, you may be able to save yourself.

The river's current is powerful, and the water is icy cold from melting snow up north. But you feel strong and determined. You swim hard for the western shore, which seems closer. Within 20 minutes, you believe you can see the outline of trees on the horizon.

Turn the page.

The Mississippi River is about 1 mile (1.6 kilometers) wide near Memphis, Tennessee.

However, a few minutes later, you realize the trees are really clouds. You're still far from the shore. Your confidence wavers, but you keep going.

Before long, you're shivering badly from the cold. You can't feel your hands or feet. Then you can't feel your arms or legs. Your brain is telling your legs to keep kicking, but you can't be sure if you are.

Your head slips under the surface, and you get a big gulp of river water in your mouth. Then you get another one. Your arm strokes are growing slower and weaker. Your heartbeat is slowing. You can't go on. You slide silently under the dark water—forever.

THE END

To follow another path, turn to page 11.
To learn more about the *Sultana* disaster,
turn to page 101.

Deserting the Army felt shameful enough. You can't ignore these people who need your help, even if you'll be punished later. At least it won't be a wartime prison camp.

You run to the end of the dock and jump into the water. You swim out to a woman who is struggling to stay afloat with her young daughter. You help the girl swim to shore while the mother follows. You swim back out and help pull in a soldier, then another. Bronson is doing the same.

The *Sultana*'s survivors are scared. Many are crying. They've all seen death up close this night. Officials from the city, including hospital workers, are helping, too.

In the dawn's light, you see many soldiers walking around town in red long underwear. They shed their wet clothes during the disaster, and the hospital provided the long johns.

Turn the page.

You notice one soldier in red long johns staring at you. He's from your unit. He can see that you are dry and wearing your uniform. He must know that you weren't on the boat. He looks angry. Will he report you?

You'll find out soon enough.

THE END

To follow another path, turn to page 11.
To learn more about the *Sultana* disaster, turn to page 101.

You just got out of a prison. You're not going to risk getting caught and going to another one.

You and Bronson return quickly to your hotel room, shut the curtains, and wait. Late the next day, you peek out the window and see that the streets are nearly empty again.

You'll have to find civilian clothes, so no one recognizes you as officers. You'll also need to get train tickets and avoid other officers. You'll have to worry about being caught—perhaps for the rest of your lives.

At least I'm alive, you tell yourself.

But deep inside, you can feel the guilt growing. You let your fellow soldiers down. Even if you make it home, you may never forgive yourself.

THE END

To follow another path, turn to page 11.
To learn more about the *Sultana* disaster, turn to page 101.

You said you would stick with Bronson, so that's what you do. You let go of the railing and jump as far as you can. You clear the lower deck and plunge into the cold water.

You come up not far from Bronson, and you swim over to him. Between his broken arm and being dazed by the blast, he doesn't look too strong right now. He's struggling to stay above water.

You cradle his head and begin to backstroke toward the shore. You swim past screaming, dying men. Everything is chaos—the noise, the flames, and the debris floating in the water.

You're starting to think you won't make it when you notice something. A piece of the ship's mast is floating upriver from you.

You tread water for a few minutes, and soon the mast floats close enough for you to grab on. You feel a wave of relief flow through your body.

Near dawn, another steamboat helped search for and rescue survivors from the river.

You sling Bronson's good arm over the mast and help hold him in place. He drifts in and out of consciousness as you hold on tight.

Finally, in the light of the dawn, you see another steamboat coming down the river. Men are working to pluck survivors out of the water. You call out, and soon they come over and help pull you out.

Turn the page.

"Thank you!" you say.

Bronson's body is badly burned, and he is still unconscious. Still, you're so relieved that you can't help but laugh. A crew member on the boat brings you a blanket, and you wrap yourself up. So many have died. It was a terrible disaster. But still, you give another small laugh. You can hardly believe you survived.

THE END

To follow another path, turn to page 11.
To learn more about the *Sultana* disaster, turn to page 101.

You and Bronson promised to stick together. But you didn't promise to die with him. You're safer here on the boat, so that's where you stay.

But it doesn't take long for the fire to spread very close to you. You choke on the thick smoke. Through blurry eyes, you see someone nearby jump into the water. You decide that's the smartest move at this point, so you follow.

However, you misjudge the distance. You don't jump far enough, and you hit the edge of the hull. Pain explodes in both your legs as your bones shatter. You black out before falling into the icy water—never to wake again.

THE END

To follow another path, turn to page 11.
To learn more about the *Sultana* disaster,
turn to page 101.

"I'm sorry, Carlson," you say. "You'll need to get off. This horse can't hold all of us."

"Sir?" he says.

"That's an order, I'm afraid," you say.

Carlson's jaw starts to tremble. But he doesn't cry. He says, "It's okay, Sir. I know you're going to be a daddy. You need to get home to that baby."

Carlson lets go of the horse and drifts away in the current. You watch him tread water for a while until he drifts away in the dark.

In the morning, you've drifted downriver back to Memphis. You, Bronson, and the horse all make it to the docks alive. You've survived. But Carlson's trembling face will haunt you for the rest of your life.

THE END

To follow another path, turn to page 11.
To learn more about the *Sultana* disaster,
turn to page 101.

You would be within your rights to pull rank on Private Carlson. But you also feel that it's your duty to keep him safe. So you let him stay on the horse with you and Bronson.

Before long, the horse begins to struggle even more. Carlson is crying—he's just a boy, you realize. You look at Bronson, who's cradling his broken arm. You know what you need to do.

You let go.

You drift away from the horse and the others and begin to swim for shore. The cold is deep in your bones now. You might freeze. You might drown. Or you might make it. You don't know what will happen. But you know that you gave the others a chance. It was the right thing to do.

THE END

To follow another path, turn to page 11.
To learn more about the *Sultana* disaster,
turn to page 101.

Many families were torn apart by the U.S. Civil War. Brothers often fought against each other in battle.

CHAPTER 4
THE TENNESSEE UNIONIST

For most people in this awful war, there was no question about what side they were on. You were either with the Union or the Confederacy. North or South. Your family, your neighbors, even your way of life—everything fit on one side or the other.

But it wasn't that way for you. In your small eastern Tennessee town, you had neighbors on both sides of the conflict. Some people started out as Unionists and became Confederates. Some did the opposite. Tennessee joined the Confederacy in 1861, but that didn't put everyone on the same page.

Turn the page.

As a younger man, you supported the South. But eventually you saw enough of the evils of slavery to change your mind. You decided to enlist in the Union Army. But your mother still supports the South. So going home is going to be strange.

It's also going to be a long trip. As a member of a Tennessee Cavalry, you were imprisoned at Cahaba Camp in Alabama—about 300 miles (483 kilometers) from your home. But you first have to travel all the way to Columbus, Ohio, to be processed and released from the Army. Only then can you travel back home. In all, your journey will be more than 1,000 miles (1,600 km).

You and three friends board the *Sultana* early in the morning. You're among the first people on the ship, so you manage to claim a small cabin near the center of the boat. You know you're lucky. The boat is so overcrowded that most people have to stand on the deck for the entire journey.

Your cabin has two doors. One leads to the interior hall. The other opens to the deck outside. After the boat leaves the harbor, you stand out on the deck and talk with a man staying in the next cabin.

His name is Hartley. His face and neck are burned. He is one of the few soldiers on board who was not a prisoner. He was burned in battle and discharged in New Orleans, where his wife and daughter met him. Now they're traveling north to stay with his parents while he recovers from his injuries.

That night, you give the room's only bed to your friend Salter. He's recovering from a gunshot wound in his stomach. You and the others sleep on the floor. It's about 2:00 a.m. when a loud crack and rumble wake you up. You sit up in the dark.

"Did you hear that?" Salter asks.

Turn the page.

"I did," you say. You quickly get dressed and open the door to the hall. But you can't see anything. The hallway is filling with black smoke. You feel the boat swaying and hear people yelling outside. Something is wrong. You're about to shut the door to your room when you hear a voice in the hall. Someone is calling for help.

To investigate the cries for help,
go to page 75.

To shut the cabin door and check the deck,
turn to page 78.

You're not going to ignore a call for help. When you step into the hall, the smoke burns your eyes, nose, and throat. You step forward carefully, holding your hands in front of you.

"Over here!"

It's Hartley, the injured soldier from next door. You feel your way to his door, and he grabs on to your jacket.

"With my injuries, I'm not strong enough to get my family to safety," he says. "I need your help."

Inside Hartley's room, his wife has put on a life preserver. There's only one other life preserver. You try to put it on the little girl, but it's too big.

Turn the page.

Steamboats were often built with a deck and railings outside passenger cabins to provide a view of the river.

"It's okay," she says to you. "I can swim." Instead, you give the preserver to Hartley.

At that moment, fire erupts outside the cabin door. You'll have to go out to the deck and jump down into the river. The four of you are about to jump when you have an idea.

"Wait. We could remove the door and take it with us," you say. "It will act as a raft."

The door would be helpful for you and the little girl. Neither of you have life preservers.

Hartley has a knife that you could use as a screwdriver. But as he fumbles for it, another wave of flames roars through the hallway.

"We don't have time!" Hartley yells.

To jump into the water now, turn to page 79.
To remove the door, turn to page 81.

You slam your cabin door to keep the smoke and flames out. Salter, Browning, and Jones are already out on the deck. Salter and Jones are wearing life preservers—the only two that were in your room.

You look over the deck. You'll have to jump out far enough to clear the main deck below and land safely in the water. If you hit the main deck, you'll probably be badly hurt.

Instead, you could try to get down to the main deck and jump from there, which might be safer. But with the fire and smoke in the hallway, you're not sure you'll make it there. Is it worth the risk?

To try to get to the lower deck, turn to page 83.

To jump from here, turn to page 84.

"You're right," you say to Hartley. "We'd better get off this boat while we still can."

"Please," Hartley says. "Will you take Madeline?"

"Yes!" you say. "I've got her."

You pick up the little girl and wrap her in your arms. "Hold on," you say to her.

Hartley and his wife hold hands and jump. You watch as they clear the main deck and land in the water. Before they come up, you follow with Madeline.

The cold air rushes past your face as you fall. It seems like you're in the air for a long time. Madeline holds on to you so tight it nearly crushes your lungs. Finally, you hit the water.

Turn the page.

The impact is hard, and you lose your grip on the little girl. You feel around for her in the water, but you can't find her.

You surface. You take two big breaths, then you dive again. With your hands outstretched in front of you, you swim down as far as you can, then up again. You do this over and over, but you never find Madeline. You don't see Hartley or his wife, either. Even your friends are lost in the chaos.

At last, you give up diving. You float on the water, calling out, "Madeline! Madeline!" But you never hear an answer.

THE END

To follow another path, turn to page 11.
To learn more about the *Sultana* disaster,
turn to page 101.

"We have to try!" you say.

You grab Hartley's knife and begin turning the doorjamb screws with the tip of the blade. It feels like it takes forever as the room fills with smoke. The girl starts to cry, and Hartley hugs her.

"It's okay, Madeline," he says.

Finally, you get the door off. With Hartley's help, you move it out onto the deck and toss it into the water.

"Now, everyone get in the water!" you say.

Mrs. Hartley jumps off the railing, but she doesn't jump far enough and hits the deck below. Several mules have broken out of their pens and are running on the deck. It looks like Mrs. Hartley is going to be trampled!

Turn the page.

Hartley and Madeline go for the stairs. But you think it'll take too long to get through the crowd to help his wife. Instead, you climb over the railing and lower yourself as far as you can. Then you drop to the deck below.

You're about to try to pull Mrs. Hartley away from the mules when you see Madeline. She's alone and crying. She can't find her parents, and she doesn't see you.

To try to save Mrs. Hartley, turn to page 86.
To help Madeline, turn to page 89.

Like you, Browning isn't wearing a life preserver. The two of you push your way toward the stairs near the front of the ship. People are running, yelling, and jumping—everything is confusing and loud. But as you get closer to the front of the boat, you notice the fire seems to fade. You seem to be safer up here.

You and Browning find the stairs and slowly push through the crowd to the lower deck. With the fire mostly at the back of the boat, you think you're safer here, at least for a while. Perhaps a rescue boat will come soon. Neither of you have life preservers. It might be smarter to wait here instead of jumping into the cold, rushing Mississippi River.

To wait where you are, turn to page 91.
To jump in and try to make it to the shore, turn to page 93.

"We can't go to the main deck," you say. "The fire is too hot. And there are too many people. We'd get caught in the crowd and never make it to the railing."

"I agree," Browning says. "We'll have to jump for it. We can do this!"

Like you, he has no life preserver. But his words give you courage. You and your cabin mates all climb on to the railing and jump out as far as you can. You manage to clear the main deck and hit the water—but hard.

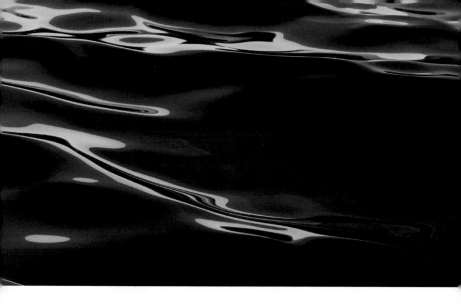

You land sideways, and the impact knocks the air out of your lungs. As you gasp in pain, you inhale some river water. You begin coughing underwater, which makes things worse.

You feel your lungs filling with icy water. Soon things begin growing darker around you. Then darker still until your life flows away like the icy water around you.

THE END

To follow another path, turn to page 11.
To learn more about the *Sultana* disaster, turn to page 101.

Madeline is lost and scared, but she's not in danger. Not yet anyway. But her mother is laying unconscious on the deck and could be trampled by the mules. That seems more important.

You rush into the pack of mules and push one away from Mrs. Hartley. It kicks you hard in the leg. The pain is brutal, but you ignore it. You grab Mrs. Hartley's wrist, pull her to her feet, and lift her over your shoulder.

"Madeline!" you yell. Amazingly, she hears you. She slips through the crowd of panicked soldiers and passengers and reaches your side. You shake Mrs. Hartley, and she wakes up.

"Aaah!" she yells, holding her side.

"You fell on to the deck," you say. "But you must be brave now. Come on!"

You take Madeline's hand and lead her to the railing and look overboard. There, just where you threw it, is the door.

"Aim to land in front of that door," you tell Madeline and her mother.

"But I want my daddy!" Madeline cries.

Just then, a burning mast cracks in half and falls on to the deck. Several men are crushed beneath it. Fire roars up the broken walls.

"We'll have to find him later," you say to Madeline.

Then the three of you climb on to the railing and jump. After landing in the water, you find the door. Madeline is already hanging on to it. You swim to her and help her get on the door.

Turn the page.

Then you look around and spot her mother. Mrs. Hartley is badly hurt and having trouble swimming. You swim out to her and pull her to the door.

You all hold on to the door and wait. The water feels like ice. You can see Madeline's skin is turning blue from the cold. The three of you float silently all the way down to Memphis. There, guards pull you from the water and take you to a hospital.

You never see your friends again. Madeline and her mother never see Hartley again either. In fact, the vast majority of those on the *Sultana* were killed. It doesn't feel like it now, but you were three of the lucky ones.

THE END

To follow another path, turn to page 11.
To learn more about the *Sultana* disaster, turn to page 101.

You can't leave that little girl all alone at a moment like this. So you shove through the crowd until you reach Madeline. As you're about to grab her hand, a burning mast crashes down onto the deck behind you. Several men are crushed, and the cracked and broken deck goes up in flames.

"Madeline!" you cry. "Madeline!"

But you've lost her. A running soldier shoves you, and you fall to the deck. Then you feel searing pain as a panicked mule kicks you in the side. You roll away from the animal, but then another soldier steps on your back.

You try to push yourself to your knees. If you can make it to the railing, you can jump into the water. But then someone trips over you, kicking your cracked ribs and knocking you down.

Turn the page.

You crawl away, but the fire from the burning mast rises in a wall in front of you.

You finally manage to stand up and turn back. But fire rages there, too. Your jacket catches fire. So does your beard. You stagger toward the railing, but the fire overwhelms you before you can jump into the water.

THE END

To follow another path, turn to page 11.
To learn more about the *Sultana* disaster,
turn to page 101.

"We're safe here for now," you say. "Let's wait and see what happens."

You and Browning stand by the railing at the very front of the boat. You watch as people struggle in the water. Looking up, you can see the outline of trees on the shore.

You wonder how far away the shore is. Maybe you could swim it. But as you watch, the trees seem to float away. Then you realize that the boat is turning in the wind. Soon you're facing the opposite direction. On this side, you cannot see the other shoreline.

More importantly, the boat is facing the opposite direction. The wind is now blowing toward the front of the boat. That means the fire is coming your way!

Turn the page.

You hear flames cracking like a whip, over and over. The cabins, rails, and decking are all crumbling as the fire makes its way toward you. The stairs are in flames as well. You, Browning, and about two dozen other men are trapped.

"Did you hear that?" Browning says.

"No," you say. "Hear what?"

"I think someone in the water is calling to us. I think it could be another boat."

"I don't hear it," you say. You peer into the distance, but you don't see any boat.

One of the other men trapped with you says that there might be more life preservers in a storeroom below deck. It's very close. You could run down and grab some.

To go get the life preservers, turn to page 96.
To listen for the voices Browning heard, turn to page 98.

"Let's get off here while we still can," you say.

You and Browning leap off the boat and hit the cold water. As you swim for the shore, you hear people crying, splashing, and coughing. You see people on fire jumping off the boat. Their bodies leave orange tracers in the dark night. It's a terrible scene.

You keep swimming. After a long time, the chaos fades. You're getting close to the riverbank. Some large trees are growing in the mud along the river, and you grab on to a branch that hangs out over the water. Browning grabs one, too.

You're shivering and can't feel your fingers, but somehow you manage to hold on. The tree trunks and branches make a thick barrier to the shore, so you decide to wait.

Turn the page.

Large trees and tree roots next to the river offered some safety for survivors of the disaster.

Other men soon join you. Before long, a dozen of you are hanging on to the trees. Someone starts singing an old song you used to sing during the war, and the rest of you join in. Then you sing another song. Everyone is trying to distract themselves from the cold and from the death and horror they've seen. Some men even begin making animal noises.

Two men seem to give in to the cold. They slip off their tree branches and float away. You think about giving up yourself—the pain is almost too much to bear. But you hold on.

In the morning, a steamer like the *Sultana* comes downstream. You all start yelling. One of the boat's crew spots you and calls out. Soon, the boat turns toward you. You're going to live to tell your terrible story.

THE END

To follow another path, turn to page 11.
To learn more about the *Sultana* disaster,
turn to page 101.

You figure you'll have to jump into the water no matter what. You'd be better off if you have a life preserver. You and a few other men head downstairs to the storeroom.

In the 1860s, life preservers on ships were often made from lightweight cork.

The smoke is very thick, and you can't see much. You feel around along the wall, looking for storage containers. The smoke makes you cough and burns your eyes. You decide to give up— you'll never find the life preservers if you can't see. You can't even breathe down here.

You turn to go back upstairs, but now you can't find your way back. Which way should you go? You call out to the other men, but they can't hear you over the raging fire. A second later, the fire bursts through the wall, and the ceiling collapses on top of you. You should have jumped into the river when you could.

THE END

To follow another path, turn to page 11.
To learn more about the *Sultana* disaster,
turn to page 101.

"We can't risk going inside," you say. "We'll burn up in there!"

Instead, you and Browning go to the railing and listen.

This time you hear a faint voice. "Hello!"

"We're here!" you yell back.

Finally, out of the darkness, a small raft appears with three men on it. You and Browning jump into the water, and the men pull you onto the raft.

"Thank you!" you say.

On the way back to shore, they pick up a few other soldiers. They let you off in the mud. Then they go back out to help more people.

As you sit in the mud, Browning starts to laugh.

"What's so funny?" you ask.

"We're on the Arkansas side of the river," he says. "Those men who saved us are Confederates. It's like we got captured again, but this time I'm happy we did."

You laugh, too. You still have a long journey home, but you know that you'll make it.

THE END

To follow another path, turn to page 11.
To learn more about the *Sultana* disaster, turn to page 101.

General Robert E. Lee surrendered to General Ulysses S. Grant at the McLean House at Appomattox Court House, Virginia.

CHAPTER 5
A TERRIBLE DISASTER

On April 9, 1865, Confederate General Robert E. Lee surrendered to Union General Ulysses S. Grant. This effectively ended the long, brutal Civil War. Prisoners on both sides were released. Union soldiers imprisoned in the South needed to go to Columbus, Ohio. There, they would be discharged from the Army before they could go home.

On April 26, 1865, the *Sultana* docked in Vicksburg, Mississippi, to repair a leaky boiler. While in port, the boat took on Union soldiers who had been in Confederate prison camps. Steamboat companies were being paid as much as $10 per person to transport the former prisoners.

That was a lot of money in 1865. The *Sultana's* captain, J. Cass Mason, decided to quickly patch the boat's leaky boiler. A complete repair would take days, and Mason didn't want to lose out on a big payday. In fact, some steamboat employees bribed Army officials to get as many passengers as possible. Mason may have done the same.

The *Sultana* was designed to carry only about 375 passengers. When it left Vicksburg, it had about 2,100 people on board—nearly six times its limit.

It had been a snowy winter in the North. As a result, the Mississippi River was flooded with icy water and flowing fast. Weighed down by its heavy load, the *Sultana* chugged north against the heavy current.

At about 2:00 a.m., 7 miles (11 km) north of Memphis, the overstressed boiler exploded. The blast led to two other boilers exploding, too. The center of the boat blew up like a volcano.

The boiler heated water to create pressurized steam that powered a steamboat's engine.

The *Sultana* explosion is the worst marine disaster in American history.

Most of the people on board were asleep. Some were killed instantly by the explosion. Others were hurled through the air to land in the cold Mississippi River.

The river was almost 5 miles (8 km) wide at that point. The people couldn't see the banks in the dark. Swimming to shore wasn't an easy task. Some people found pieces of the broken boat floating in the river to hold on to. Some held on to horses or mules that had escaped the boat.

One teenage boy floated all the way back to Memphis, where he reported the disaster. Early in the morning of April 27, boats went out to rescue anyone they could. Many survivors were brought to hospitals in Memphis.

Of the roughly 2,100 people on board the *Sultana*, about 1,800 were killed. Even more people died in this event than the sinking of the *Titanic* in 1912.

MORE ABOUT THE
SULTANA

The *Sultana* was a 260-foot- (79-meter-) long wooden steamboat built in 1863. It traveled the Mississippi River between St. Louis and New Orleans, transporting passengers and freight. Steamboats were powered by steam, which was created in chambers, or boilers, where fires heated water. Pressure from the steam turned big water wheels that propelled the boat.

Jack Staff—a mast at the point of the bow, used for displaying a flag or banner, that provides the pilot with a point of reference for steering the boat

Pilothouse—the small, glassed-in structure atop the boat from which the captain or pilot steers the vessel

Bow—the front of the ship or boat

Roof Bell—used by the captain or pilot to communicate with the engineer room below on the hurricane deck

Wheel—paddle wheel located at the side of the ship, used to move the boat through the water

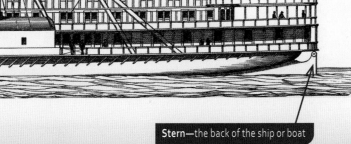

Hurricane Deck—the uppermost deck on the boat, where the pilothouse is often located

Boiler Deck—the deck above the main deck, where most passenger cabins are located

Main Deck—the lowest deck of a steamboat, where the boilers, engines and most machinery is located.

Stacks—vertical pipes used to vent steam and smoke from the boat's engines

Hull—the watertight body of a ship or boat

Mast—a vertical pole on a ship that supports sails or rigging

Stern—the back of the ship or boat

OTHER PATHS TO EXPLORE

>>> During rescue efforts after the *Sultana* blew up, many people pitched in to help. Some Union soldiers were saved by Confederates. How would it feel to trust someone who would have tried to kill you just a few weeks earlier? How would you feel if you saw your former enemy in danger? Would you try to save them? Why or why not?

>>> The captain of the *Sultana* overloaded the boat and didn't properly repair the leaky boiler. Doing so put people's lives in danger. He did it to make money. On the other hand, the soldiers and former prisoners badly wanted to go home. They would have had to wait longer if the *Sultana* hadn't taken them. Do you think the *Sultana's* captain took a reasonable risk? The captain was killed in the disaster. But if he hadn't died, should he have been punished? Why or why not?

>>> During the Civil War, doctors didn't understand how dirt and germs caused infections and disease. Many people who had injuries would have a limb amputated if their wounds were badly infected. What would it be like to see people suffer and die from what would be minor injuries today?

BIBLIOGRAPHY

American Battlefield Trust: The Sultana Disaster, https://www.battlefields.org/learn/articles/sultana-disaster.

Hamilton, Jon. "The Shipwreck That Led Confederate Veterans To Risk All For Union Lives." NPR, April 27, 2015, https://www.npr.org/2015/04/27/402515205/the-shipwreck-that-led-confederate-veterans-to-risk-all-for-union-lives.

Huffman, Alan. "Surviving the Worst: The Wreck of the Sultana at the End of the American Civil War," *Mississippi History Now,* October 2009, https://www.mshistorynow.mdah.ms.gov/issue/surviving-the-worst-the-wreck-of-the-sultana.

Knoxville History Project. "Knoxville's Nearly Forgotten Memorial to America's Deadliest Maritime Disaster, the Sultana." April 29, 2015, https://knoxvillehistoryproject.org/2015/04/29/knoxvilles-nearly-forgotten-memorial-to-americas-deadliest-maritime-disaster-the-sultana/.

National Park Service. *History of the Andersonville Prison* https://www.nps.gov/ande/learn/historyculture/camp_sumter_history.htm.

GLOSSARY

blackmail (BLAK-mayl)—to threaten to turn someone in to the authorities in exchange for money

cavalry (KA-vuhl-ree)—soldiers who travel and fight on horseback

Confederate (kuhn-FEH-duh-ruht)—having to do with the Confederate States of America during the U.S. Civil War

hurricane deck (HUHR-uh-kayn DEK)—the top deck of a passenger boat, with a roof supported by small posts

lieutenant (loo-TEH-nuhnt)—a low-ranking officer in the armed forces

maggot (MA-guht)—the larva of certain flies, often found in the bodies of decaying animals

pilothouse (PY-luht-hows)—an enclosed room where a boat's controls are located, including the steering wheel, compass, and navigation equipment

quinine (KWY-nyne)—a bitter white substance taken from the chinchona tree; used to treat certain diseases

refugee (reh-fyoo-JEE)—someone who has to leave a place to escape war or other disaster

Union (YOON-yuhn)—the Northern states that fought against the South in the U.S. Civil War

vigilant (VIH-juh-luhnt)—awake and watchful for danger

READ MORE

Berglund, Bruce. *Drummer Boys Lead the Charge: Courageous Kids of the Civil War.* North Mankato, MN: Capstone Press, 2020.

Parker, Phillip. *The Civil War Visual Encyclopedia.* New York: DK Publishing, 2021.

Smith, Elliott. *Hidden Heroes in the Civil War.* Minneapolis: Lerner Publications, 2023.

Walker, Sally M. *Sinking the Sultana: A Civil War Story of Imprisonment, Greed, and a Doomed Journey Home.* Somerville, MA: Candlewick Press, 2017.

INTERNET SITES

American Battlefield Trust: The Sultana Disaster
battlefields.org/learn/articles/sultana-disaster

National Park Service: History of the Andersonville Prison
nps.gov/ande/learn/historyculture/camp_sumter_history.htm

The Sultana Disaster Museum: Stories from the Sultana
sultanadisastermuseum.com/stories-from-the-sultana

ABOUT THE AUTHOR

Eric Braun is a children's author and editor. He has written dozens of books on many topics, and one of his books was read by an astronaut on the International Space Station for kids on Earth to watch.

Photo Credits
Alamy: Glasshouse Images, 40, Niday Picture Library, cover, 28, Reading Room 2020, 20; Bridgeman Images: Everett Collection, 12, Peter Newark American Pictures, 45; Getty Images: Bettmann, 6, 9, 17, Campwillowlake, 65, Grafissimo, 94, ivan-96, 59, MPI, 25, 100, Paul Popper/Popperfoto, 51, THEPALMER, 76, The Print Collector, 96, Universal History Archive , 70, via Corbis, 38, ZU_09, 106-107; Science Source: CLAUS LUNAU, 104; Shutterstock: Graphic Compressor, 84, Nicku, 103, Triff, 33